ANIMAL MASTERMINDS

Pod Protection!

Supersmart Dolphins

BY SARAH EASON
ILLUSTRATED BY DIEGO VAISBERG

BEARPORT
PUBLISHING

Minneapolis, Minnesota

Credits: 20, © vkilikov/Shutterstock; 21, © Matt A. Claiborne/Shutterstock; 22, © RaksyBH/Shutterstock; 23, © Subphoto.com/Shutterstock.

Bearport Publishing Company Product Development Team
President: Jen Jenson; Director of Product Development: Spencer Brinker; Senior Editor: Allison Juda; Editor: Charly Haley; Associate Editor: Naomi Reich; Senior Designer: Colin O'Dea; Associate Designer: Elena Klinkner; Associate Designer: Kayla Eggert; Product Development Assistant: Anita Stasson

Produced by Calcium
Editor: Jennifer Sanderson; Proofreader: Harriet McGregor; Designer: Paul Myerscough; Picture Researcher: Rachel Blount

DISCLAIMER: This graphic story is a dramatization based on true events. It is intended to give the reader a sense of the narrative rather than a presentation of actual details as they occurred.

Library of Congress Cataloging-in-Publication Data

Names: Eason, Sarah, author. | Vaisberg, Diego, illustrator.
Title: Pod protection! : supersmart dolphins / by Sarah Eason ; illustrated by Diego Vaisberg.
Description: Bear claw books | Minneapolis, Minnesota : Bearport Publishing Company, [2023] | Series: Animal masterminds | Includes bibliographical references and index.
Identifiers: LCCN 2022033476 (print) | LCCN 2022033477 (ebook) | ISBN 9798885094344 (library binding) | ISBN 9798885095563 (paperback) | ISBN 9798885096713 (ebook)
Subjects: LCSH: Dolphins--Behavior--Juvenile literature. | Dolphins--Behavior--Comic books, strips, etc. | Animal intelligence--Juvenile literature. | Animal intelligence--Comic books, strips, etc. | Human-animal relationships--Juvenile literature. | Human-animal relationships--Comic books, strips, etc. | LCGFT: Graphic novels.
Classification: LCC QL737.C432 E225 2023 (print) | LCC QL737.C432 (ebook) | DDC 599.5315--dc23/eng/20220830
LC record available at https://lccn.loc.gov/2022033476
LC ebook record available at https://lccn.loc.gov/2022033477

For more information, write to Bearport Publishing, 5357 Penn Avenue South, Minneapolis, MN 55419.

Contents

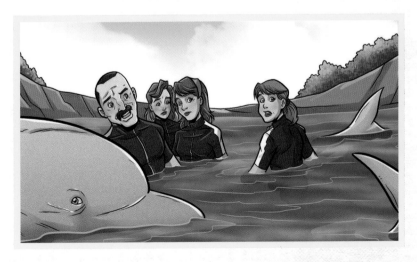

CHAPTER 1

Training Day

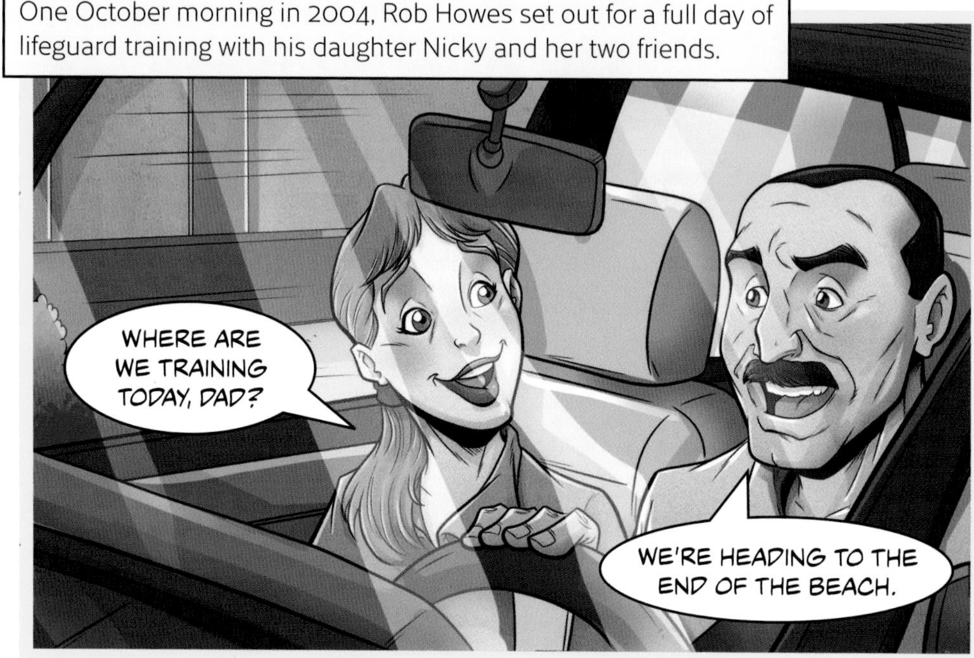
One October morning in 2004, Rob Howes set out for a full day of lifeguard training with his daughter Nicky and her two friends.
WHERE ARE WE TRAINING TODAY, DAD?
WE'RE HEADING TO THE END OF THE BEACH.

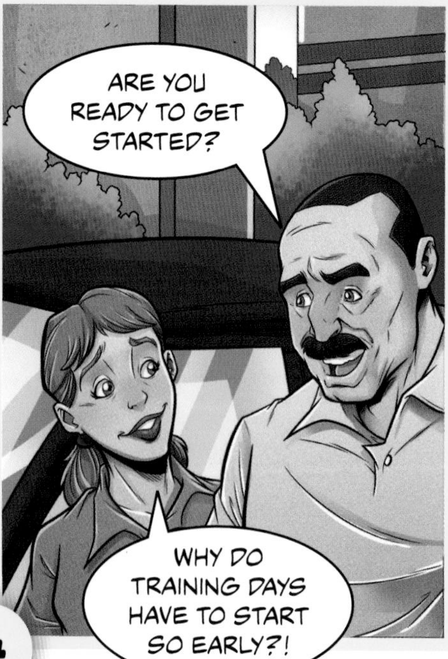
ARE YOU READY TO GET STARTED?
WHY DO TRAINING DAYS HAVE TO START SO EARLY?!

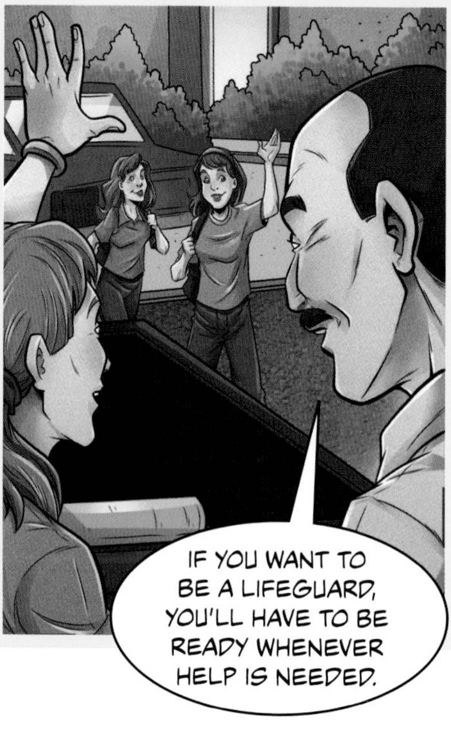
IF YOU WANT TO BE A LIFEGUARD, YOU'LL HAVE TO BE READY WHENEVER HELP IS NEEDED.

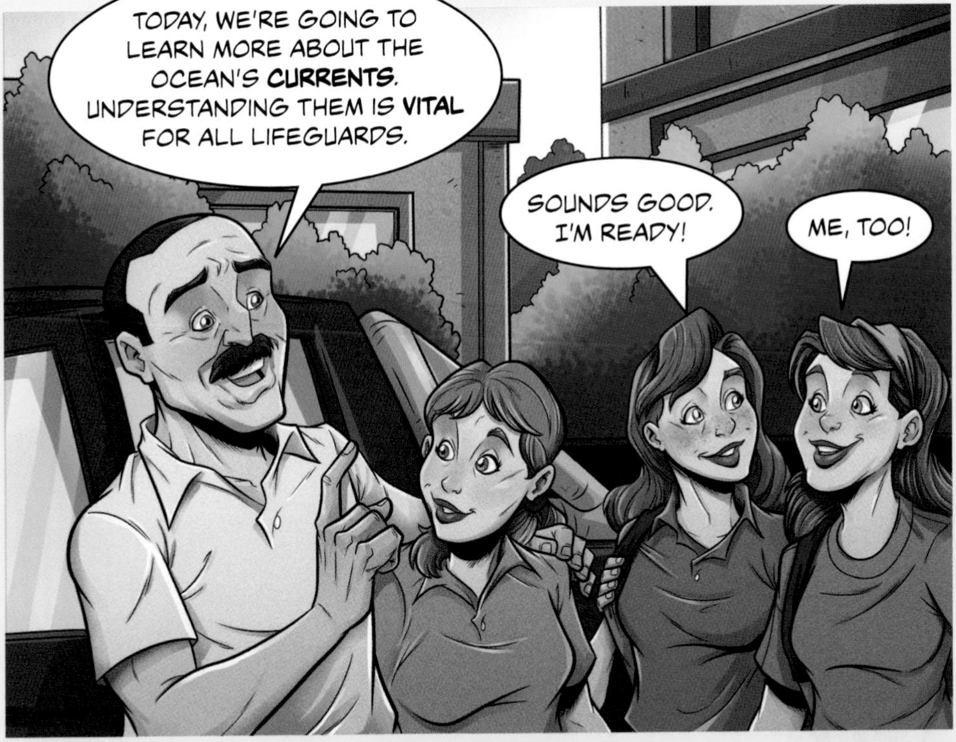
TODAY, WE'RE GOING TO LEARN MORE ABOUT THE OCEAN'S **CURRENTS**. UNDERSTANDING THEM IS **VITAL** FOR ALL LIFEGUARDS.
SOUNDS GOOD. I'M READY!
ME, TOO!

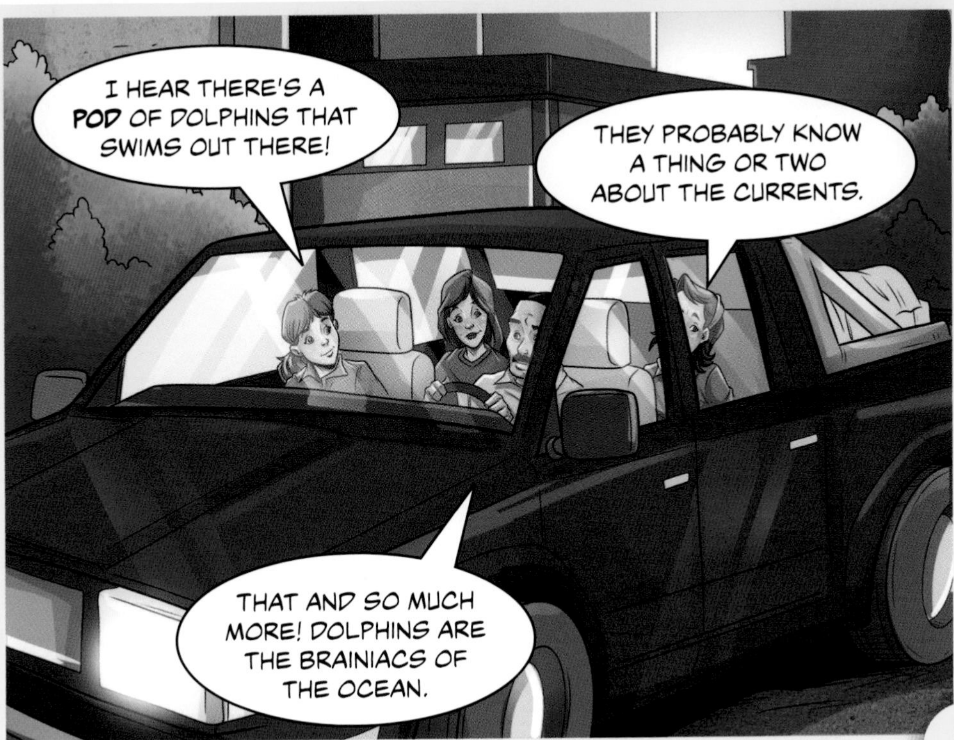
I HEAR THERE'S A **POD** OF DOLPHINS THAT SWIMS OUT THERE!
THEY PROBABLY KNOW A THING OR TWO ABOUT THE CURRENTS.
THAT AND SO MUCH MORE! DOLPHINS ARE THE BRAINIACS OF THE OCEAN.

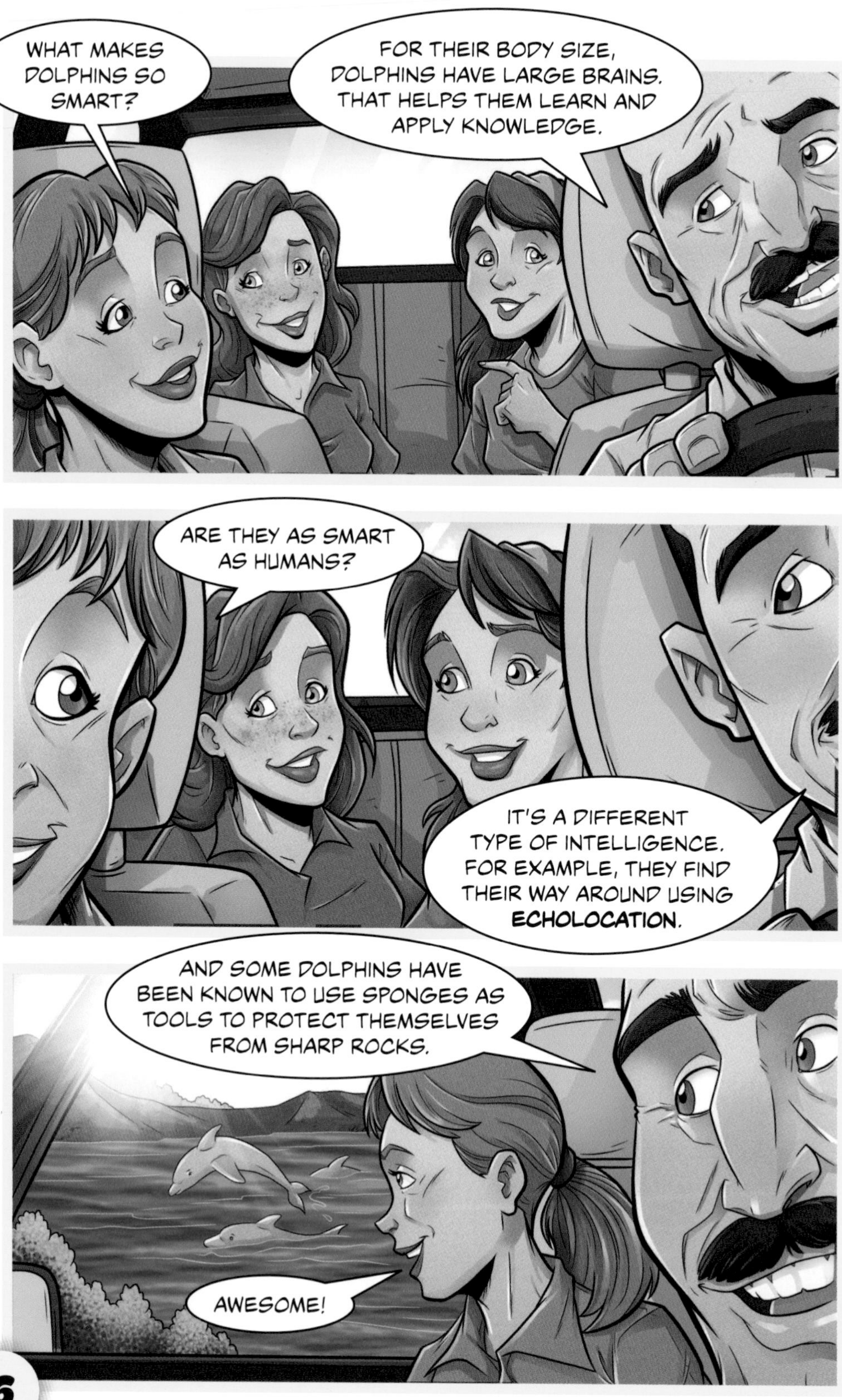
WHAT MAKES DOLPHINS SO SMART?
FOR THEIR BODY SIZE, DOLPHINS HAVE LARGE BRAINS. THAT HELPS THEM LEARN AND APPLY KNOWLEDGE.
ARE THEY AS SMART AS HUMANS?
IT'S A DIFFERENT TYPE OF INTELLIGENCE. FOR EXAMPLE, THEY FIND THEIR WAY AROUND USING **ECHOLOCATION**.
AND SOME DOLPHINS HAVE BEEN KNOWN TO USE SPONGES AS TOOLS TO PROTECT THEMSELVES FROM SHARP ROCKS.
AWESOME!

The group arrived at the beach and ran down to the water.

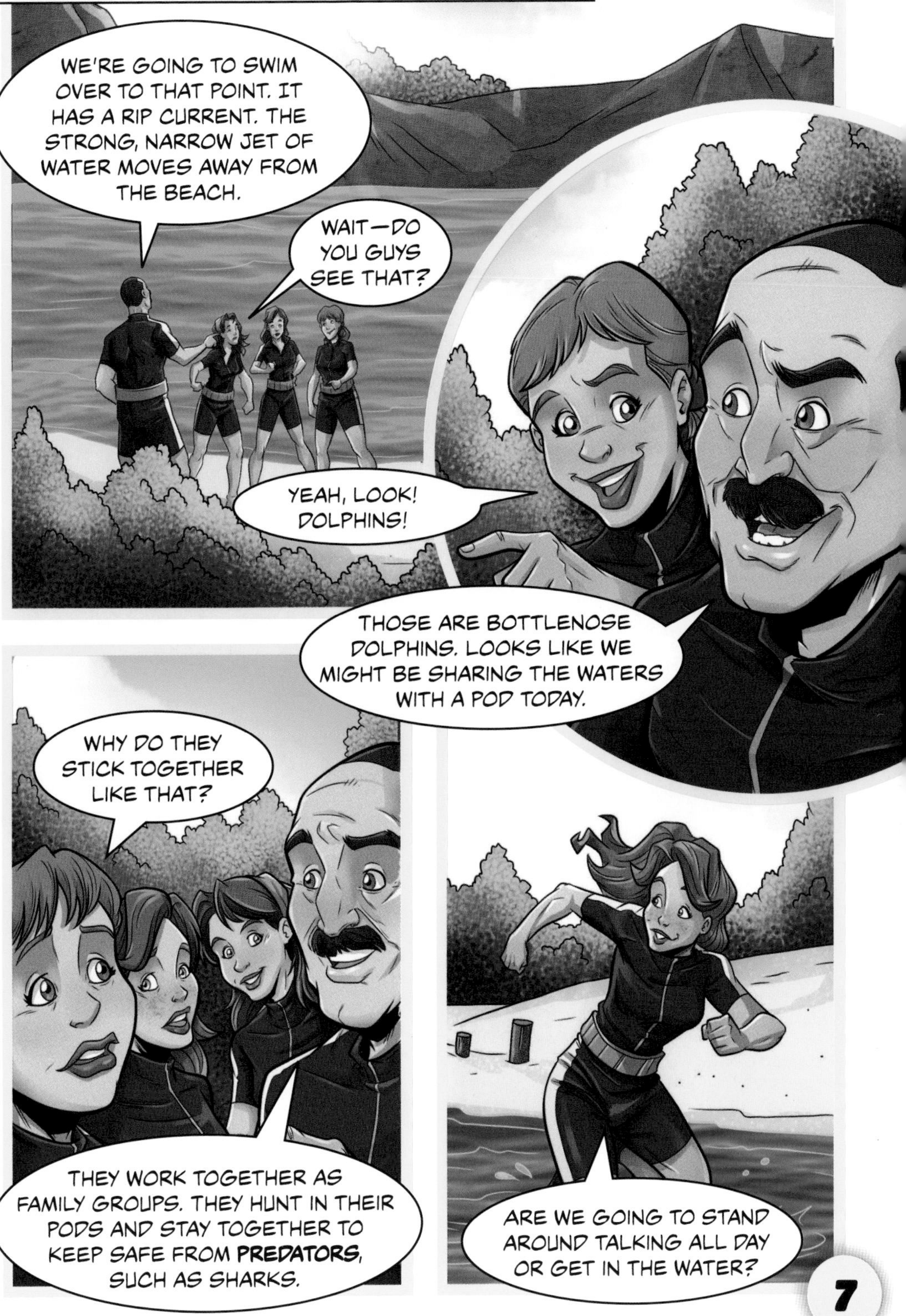
WE'RE GOING TO SWIM OVER TO THAT POINT. IT HAS A RIP CURRENT. THE STRONG, NARROW JET OF WATER MOVES AWAY FROM THE BEACH.
WAIT—DO YOU GUYS SEE THAT?
YEAH, LOOK! DOLPHINS!
THOSE ARE BOTTLENOSE DOLPHINS. LOOKS LIKE WE MIGHT BE SHARING THE WATERS WITH A POD TODAY.
WHY DO THEY STICK TOGETHER LIKE THAT?
THEY WORK TOGETHER AS FAMILY GROUPS. THEY HUNT IN THEIR PODS AND STAY TOGETHER TO KEEP SAFE FROM **PREDATORS**, SUCH AS SHARKS.
ARE WE GOING TO STAND AROUND TALKING ALL DAY OR GET IN THE WATER?

CHAPTER 2

Rounded Up

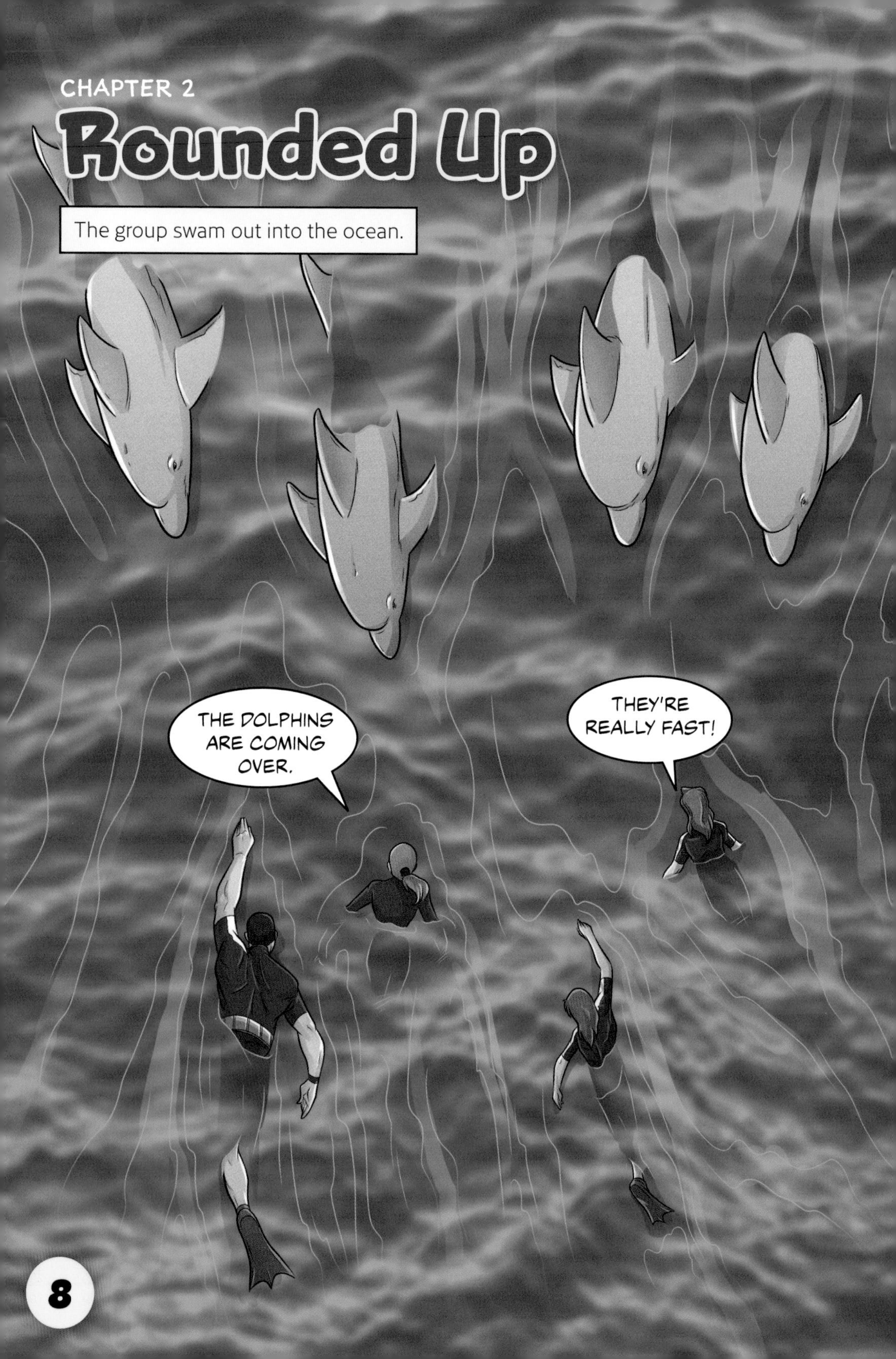
The group swam out into the ocean.
THE DOLPHINS ARE COMING OVER.
THEY'RE REALLY FAST!

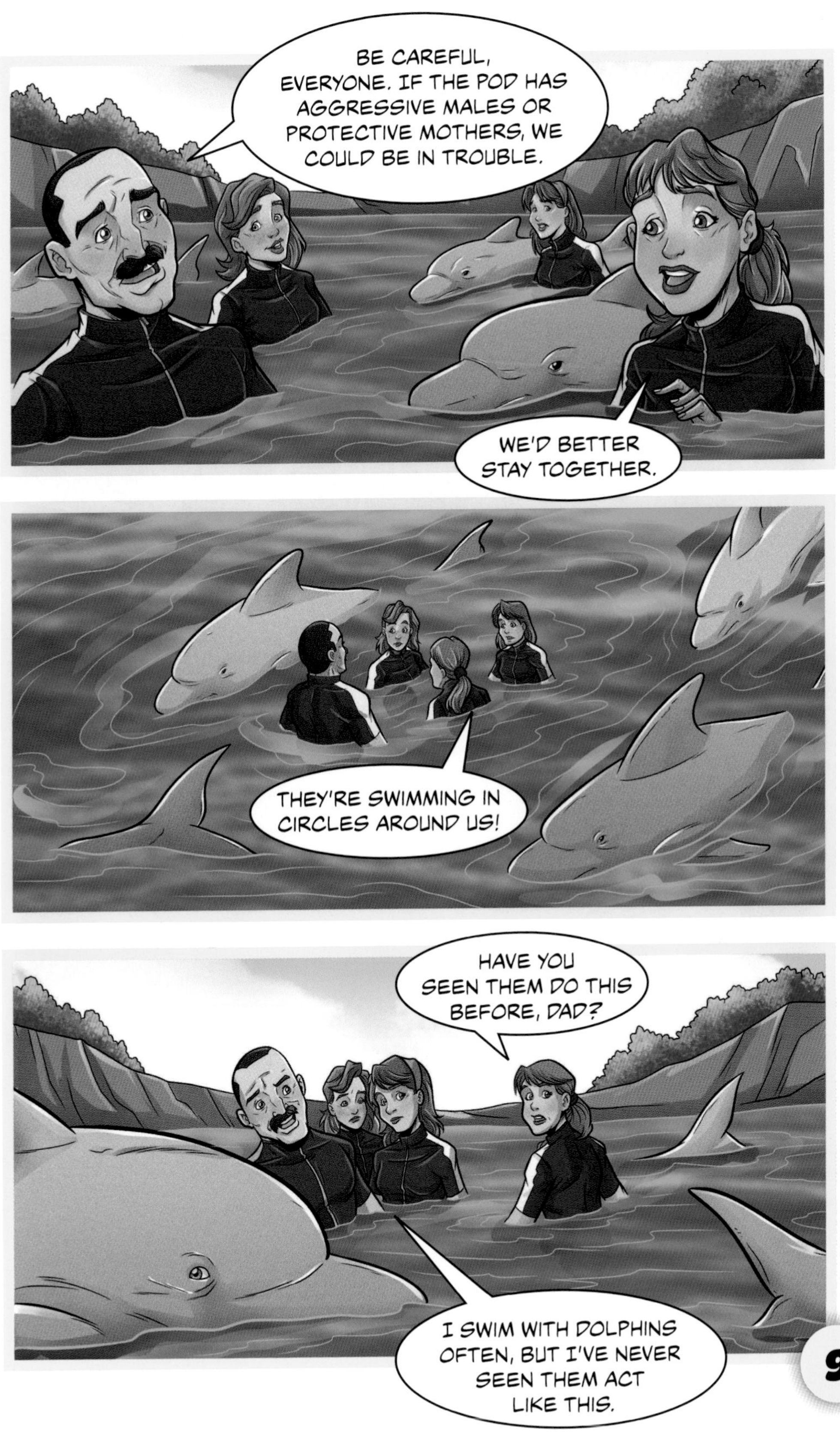
BE CAREFUL, EVERYONE. IF THE POD HAS AGGRESSIVE MALES OR PROTECTIVE MOTHERS, WE COULD BE IN TROUBLE.
WE'D BETTER STAY TOGETHER.
THEY'RE SWIMMING IN CIRCLES AROUND US!
HAVE YOU SEEN THEM DO THIS BEFORE, DAD?
I SWIM WITH DOLPHINS OFTEN, BUT I'VE NEVER SEEN THEM ACT LIKE THIS.

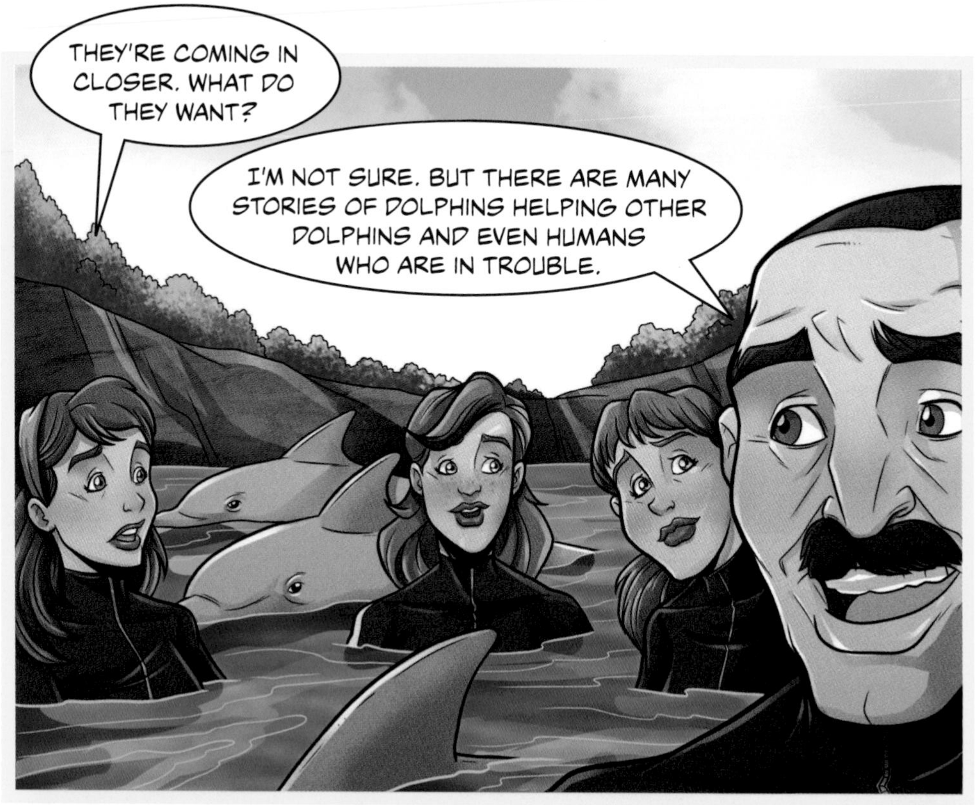
THEY'RE COMING IN CLOSER. WHAT DO THEY WANT?
I'M NOT SURE. BUT THERE ARE MANY STORIES OF DOLPHINS HELPING OTHER DOLPHINS AND EVEN HUMANS WHO ARE IN TROUBLE.

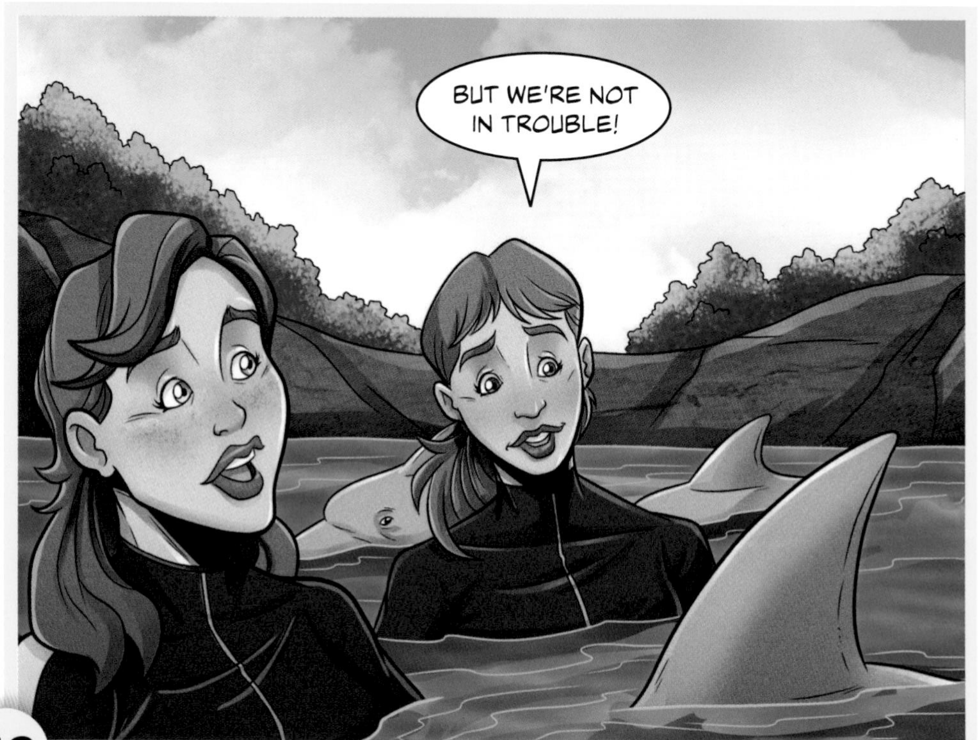
BUT WE'RE NOT IN TROUBLE!

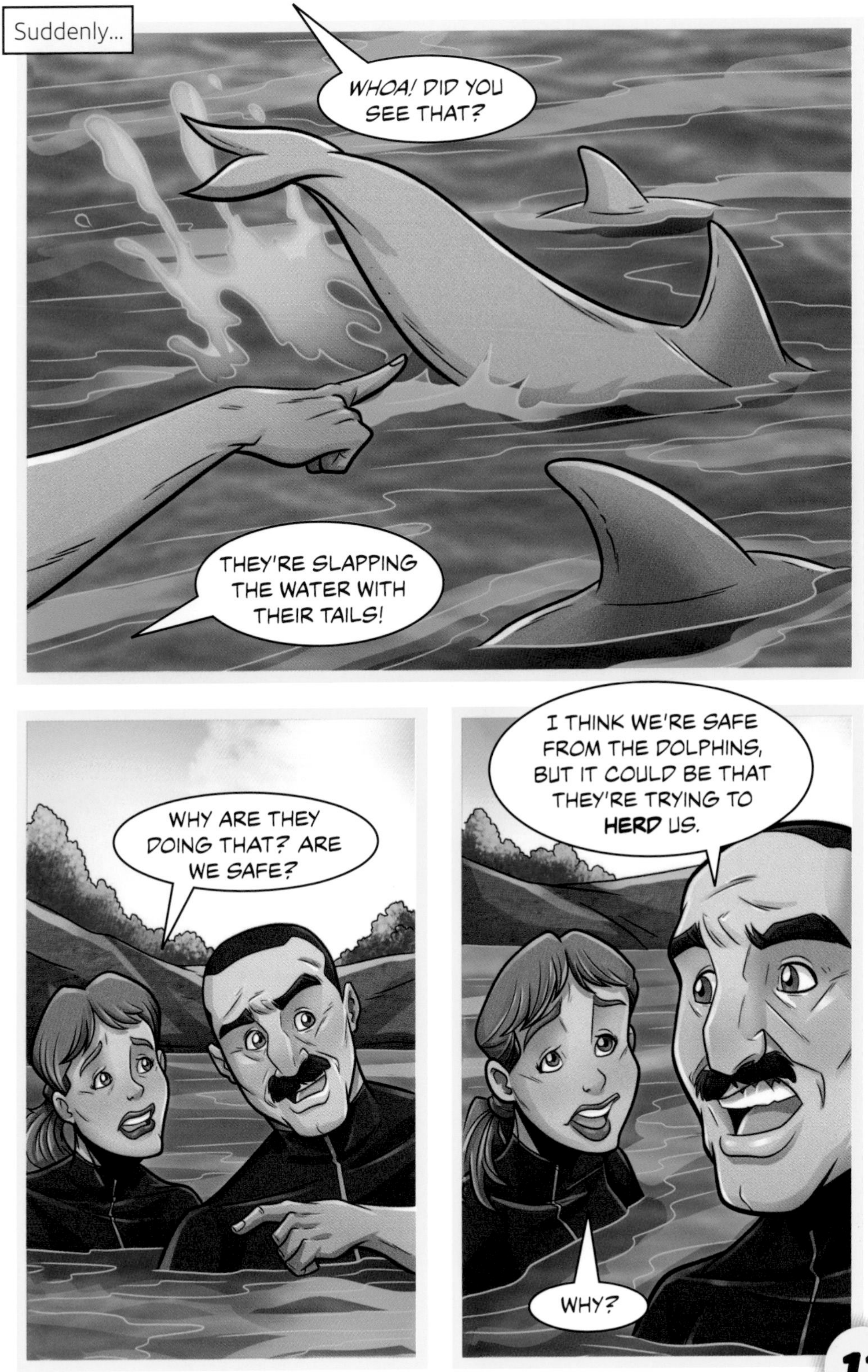

Suddenly...
WHOA! DID YOU SEE THAT?
THEY'RE SLAPPING THE WATER WITH THEIR TAILS!
WHY ARE THEY DOING THAT? ARE WE SAFE?
I THINK WE'RE SAFE FROM THE DOLPHINS, BUT IT COULD BE THAT THEY'RE TRYING TO **HERD** US.
WHY?

The lifeguards were confused and starting to worry.

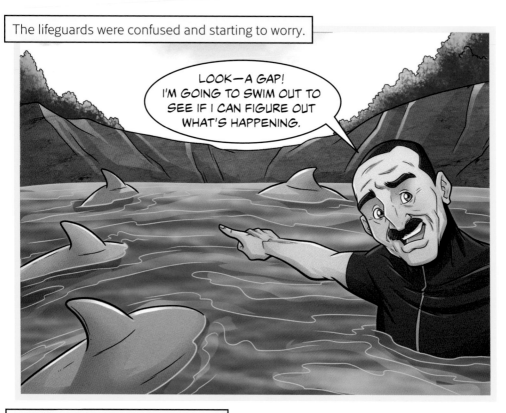

LOOK—A GAP!
I'M GOING TO SWIM OUT TO
SEE IF I CAN FIGURE OUT
WHAT'S HAPPENING.

Just then, one of the dolphins swam straight at Rob, only to dive underneath him at the last moment.

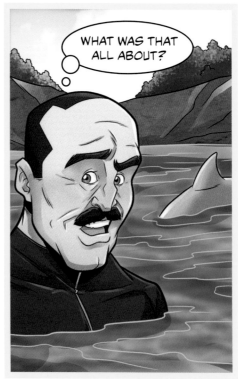

WHAT WAS THAT
ALL ABOUT?

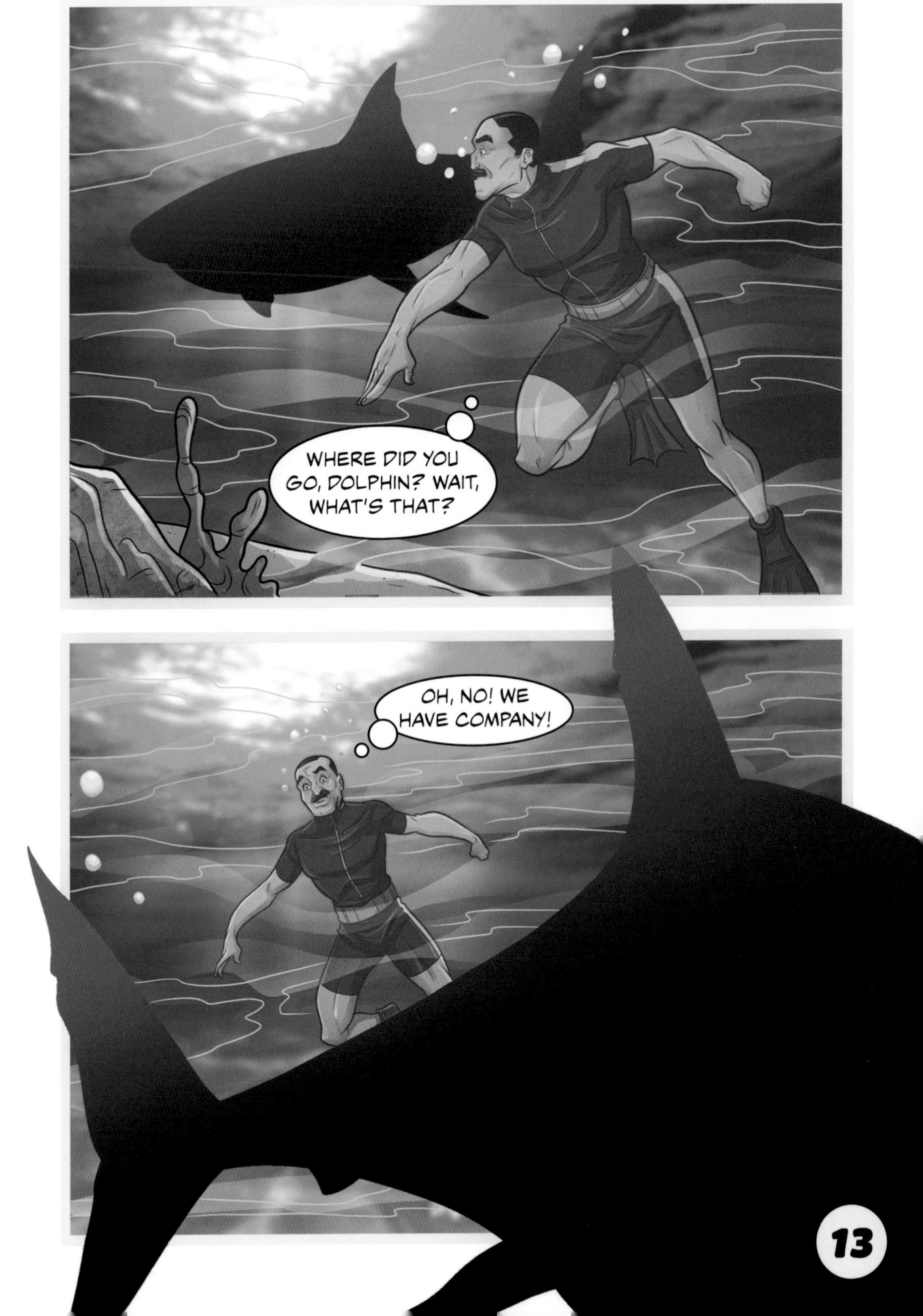
WHERE DID YOU GO, DOLPHIN? WAIT, WHAT'S THAT?
OH, NO! WE HAVE COMPANY!

CHAPTER 3

Shark Threat!

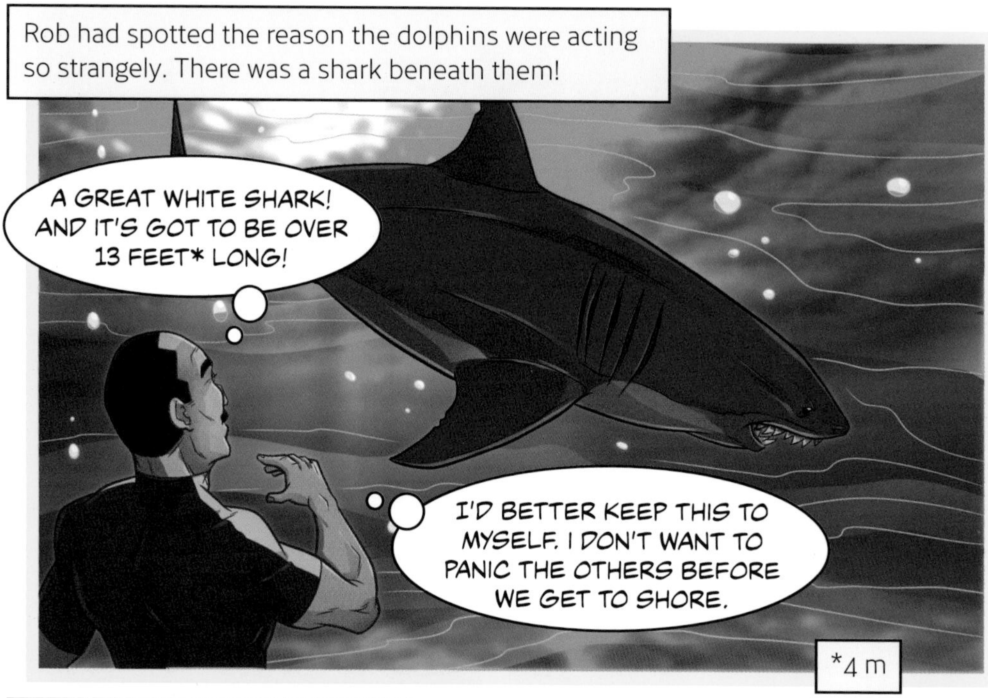
Rob had spotted the reason the dolphins were acting so strangely. There was a shark beneath them!
A GREAT WHITE SHARK! AND IT'S GOT TO BE OVER 13 FEET* LONG!
I'D BETTER KEEP THIS TO MYSELF. I DON'T WANT TO PANIC THE OTHERS BEFORE WE GET TO SHORE.
*4 m

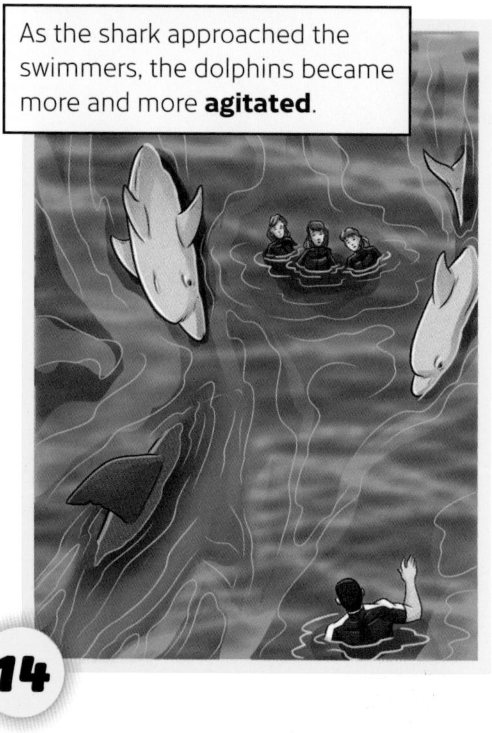
As the shark approached the swimmers, the dolphins became more and more **agitated**.

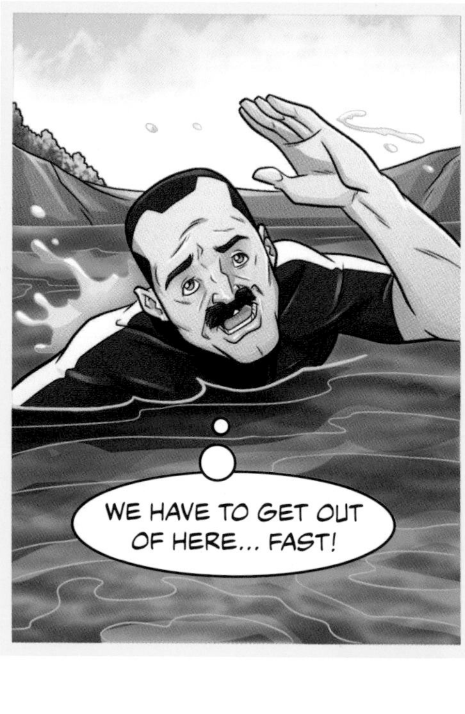
WE HAVE TO GET OUT OF HERE... FAST!

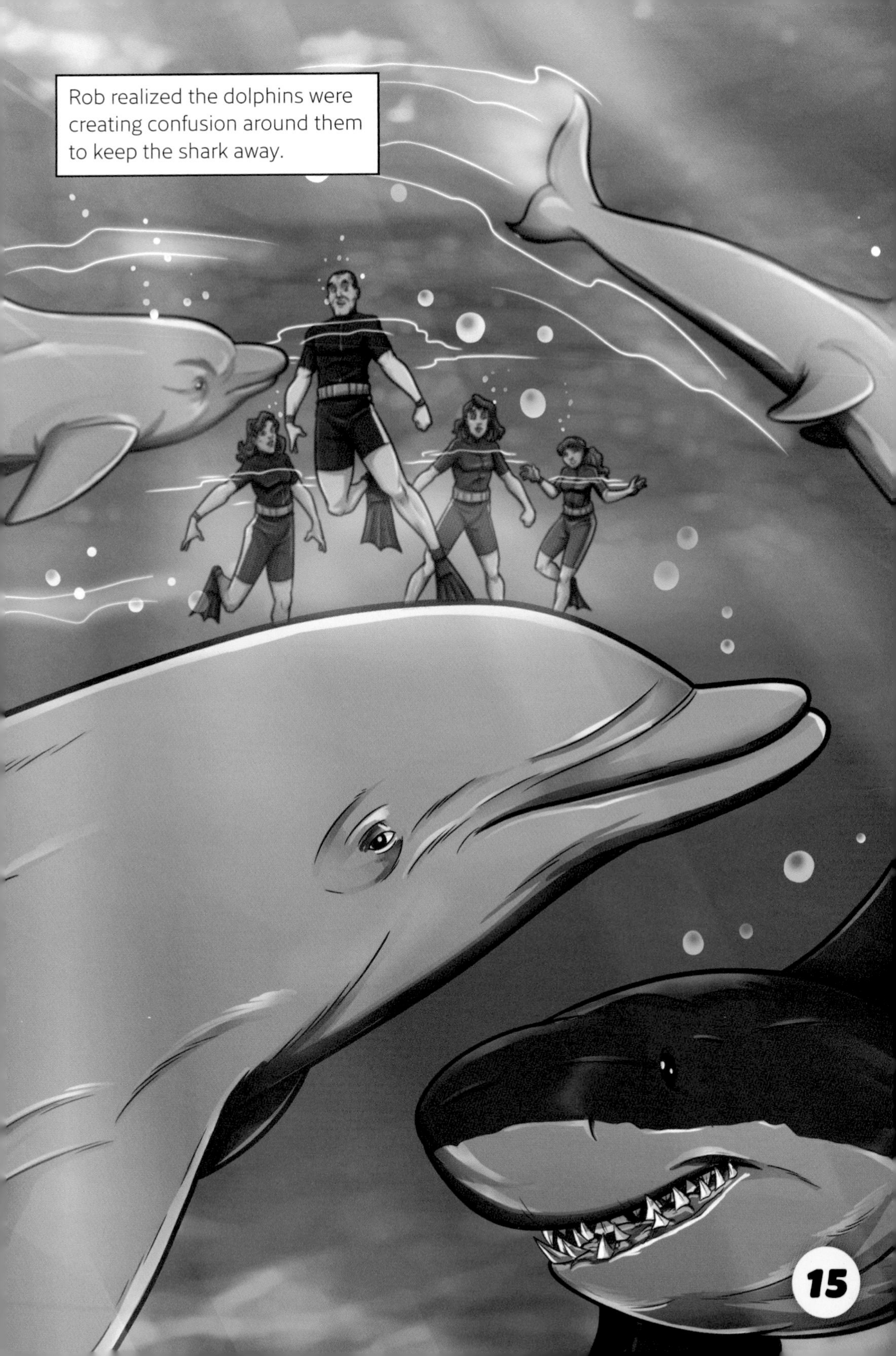
Rob realized the dolphins were creating confusion around them to keep the shark away.

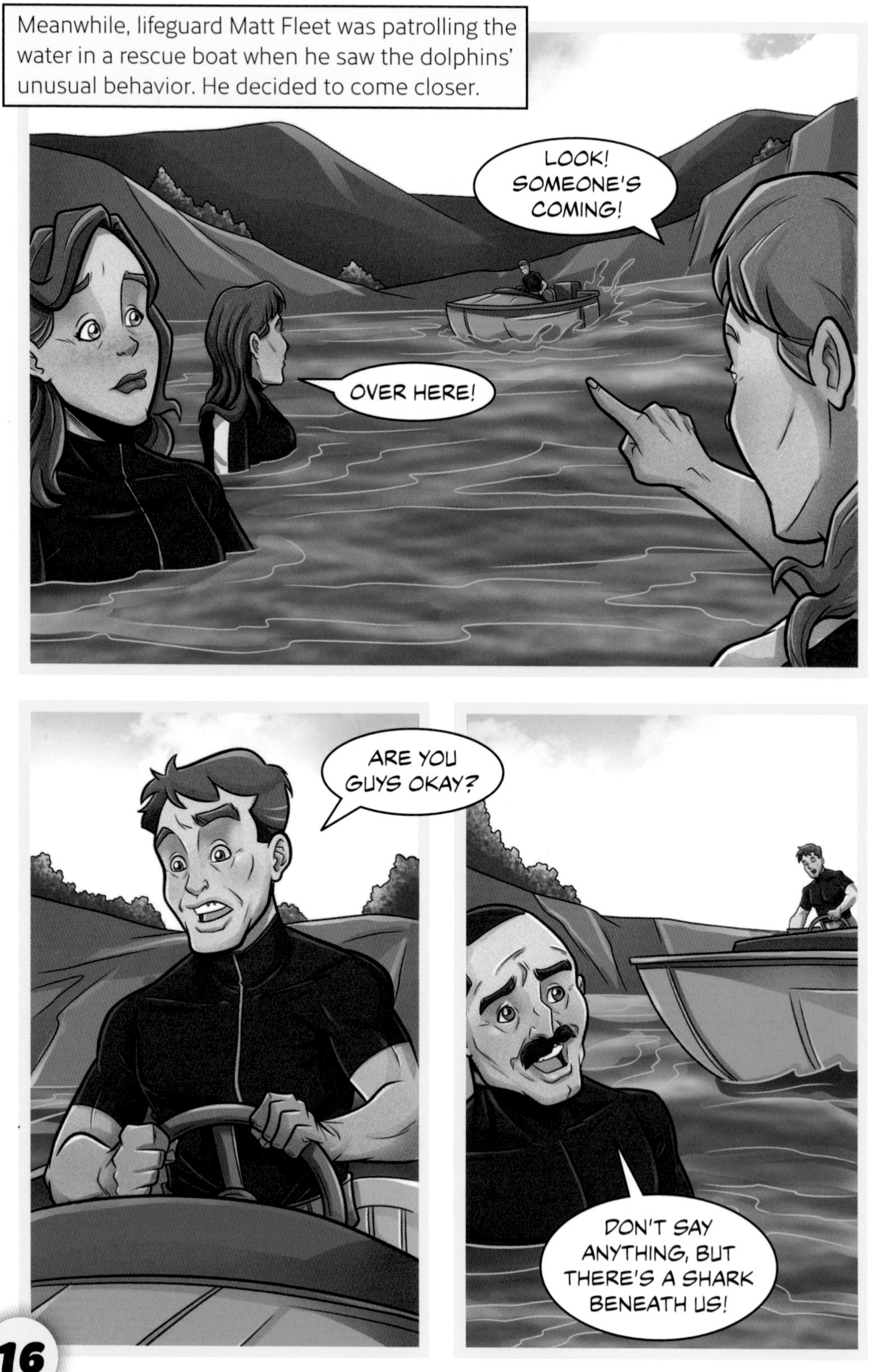
Meanwhile, lifeguard Matt Fleet was patrolling the water in a rescue boat when he saw the dolphins' unusual behavior. He decided to come closer.
LOOK! SOMEONE'S COMING!
OVER HERE!
ARE YOU GUYS OKAY?
DON'T SAY ANYTHING, BUT THERE'S A SHARK BENEATH US!

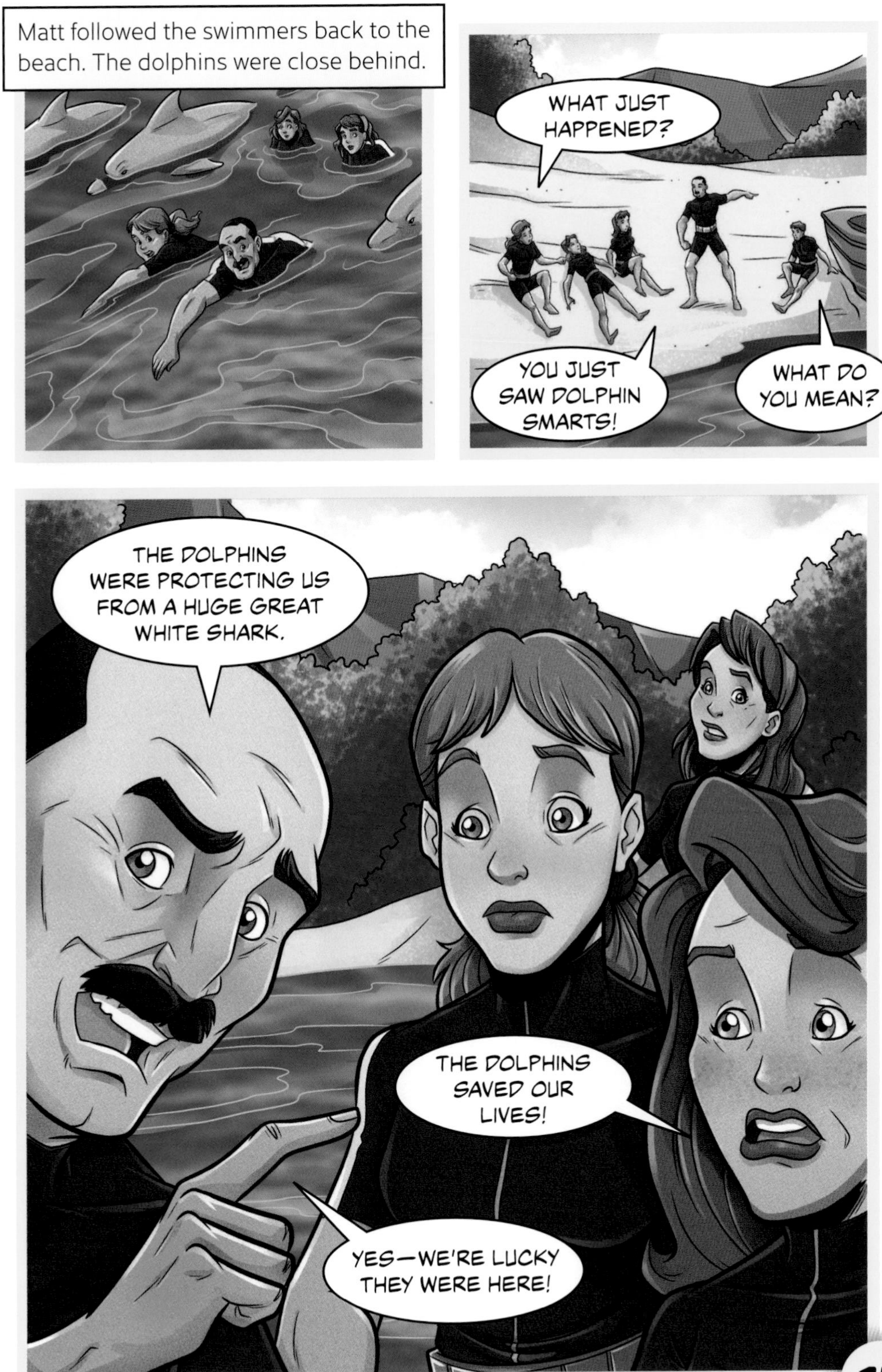
Matt followed the swimmers back to the beach. The dolphins were close behind.
WHAT JUST HAPPENED?
YOU JUST SAW DOLPHIN SMARTS!
WHAT DO YOU MEAN?
THE DOLPHINS WERE PROTECTING US FROM A HUGE GREAT WHITE SHARK.
THE DOLPHINS SAVED OUR LIVES!
YES—WE'RE LUCKY THEY WERE HERE!

CHAPTER 4

Saved by Dolphins

Soon, news of the **ordeal** spread. A few days later, Rob got a call from Dr. Rochelle Constantine, of the Auckland University School of Biological Sciences.

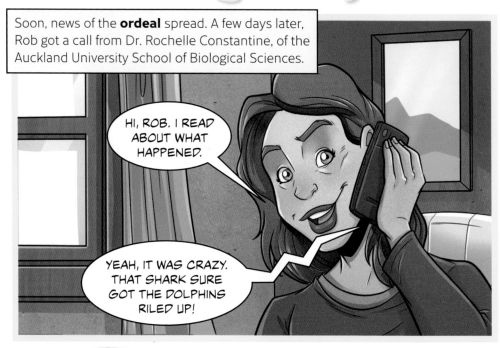

HI, ROB. I READ ABOUT WHAT HAPPENED.

YEAH, IT WAS CRAZY. THAT SHARK SURE GOT THE DOLPHINS RILED UP!

SHARKS AREN'T USUALLY A THREAT TO BOTTLENOSE DOLPHINS IN YOUR AREA.

THEN WHY DID THE DOLPHINS BEHAVE THAT WAY?

WELL, WE KNOW DOLPHINS CAN UNDERSTAND WHAT MIGHT HAPPEN WHEN A SHARK IS AROUND. AND THEY ARE SMART ENOUGH TO KNOW THAT HUMANS ARE **VULNERABLE.**

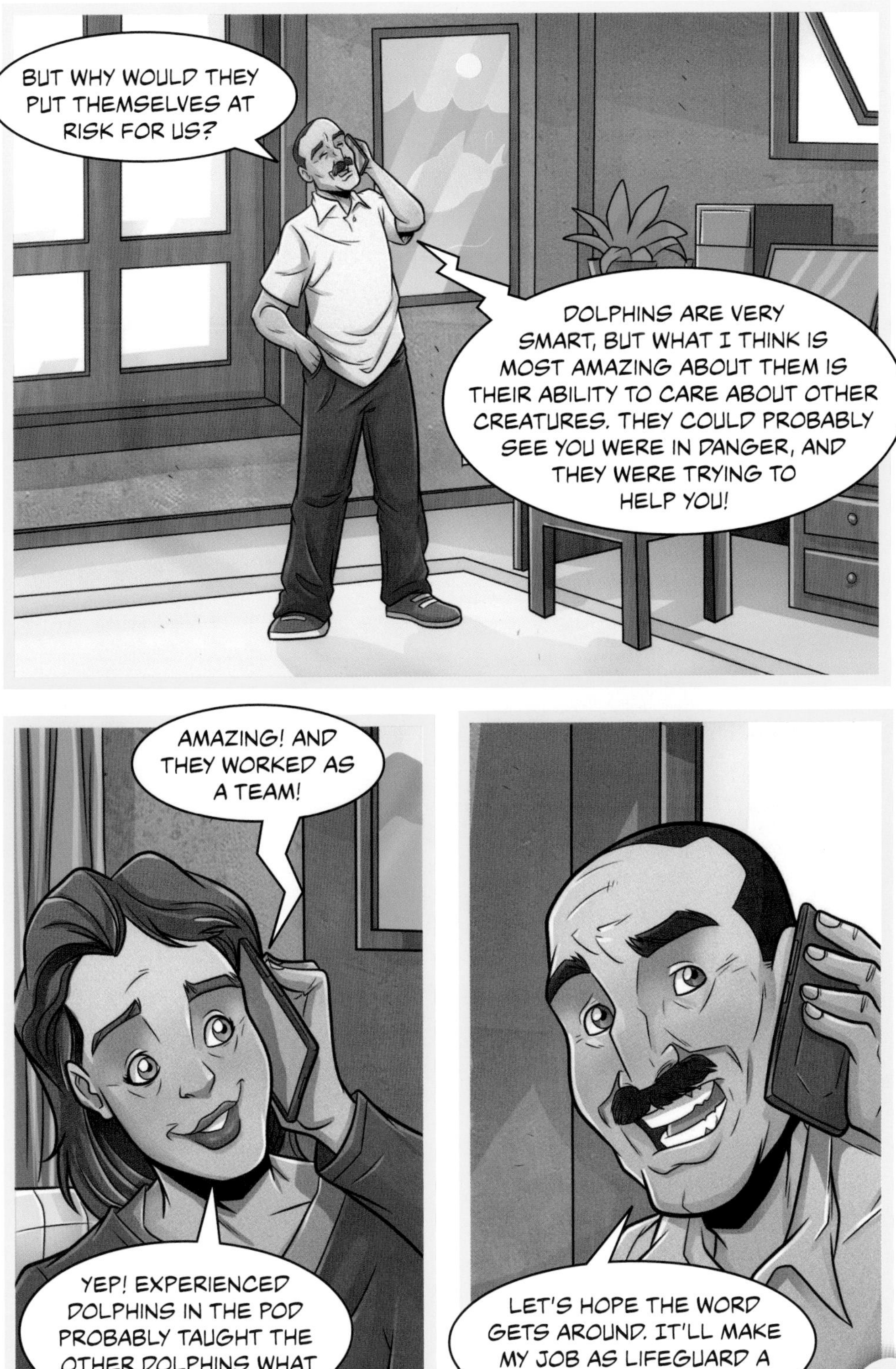

BUT WHY WOULD THEY PUT THEMSELVES AT RISK FOR US?
DOLPHINS ARE VERY SMART, BUT WHAT I THINK IS MOST AMAZING ABOUT THEM IS THEIR ABILITY TO CARE ABOUT OTHER CREATURES. THEY COULD PROBABLY SEE YOU WERE IN DANGER, AND THEY WERE TRYING TO HELP YOU!
AMAZING! AND THEY WORKED AS A TEAM!
YEP! EXPERIENCED DOLPHINS IN THE POD PROBABLY TAUGHT THE OTHER DOLPHINS WHAT TO DO.
LET'S HOPE THE WORD GETS AROUND. IT'LL MAKE MY JOB AS LIFEGUARD A WHOLE LOT EASIER!

All about Dolphins

Dolphins are some of the most intelligent animals on Earth. They are sometimes called the dogs of the sea because they are so smart and playful. Here are some more facts about these supersmart animals.

- Dolphins may look like large fish, but they are **mammals**.

- Like all mammals, dolphins breathe air. They must come to the surface of the water to breathe through blowholes on the top of their heads.

- Most dolphins live in oceans, but some live in rivers. River dolphins are found in South America and Asia.

FEMALE DOLPHINS GIVE BIRTH TO A SINGLE BABY AT A TIME. IT IS CALLED A CALF.

DOLPHINS USE THEIR TEETH TO CATCH FISH. BUT THEN THEY SWALLOW THEIR MEALS WHOLE.

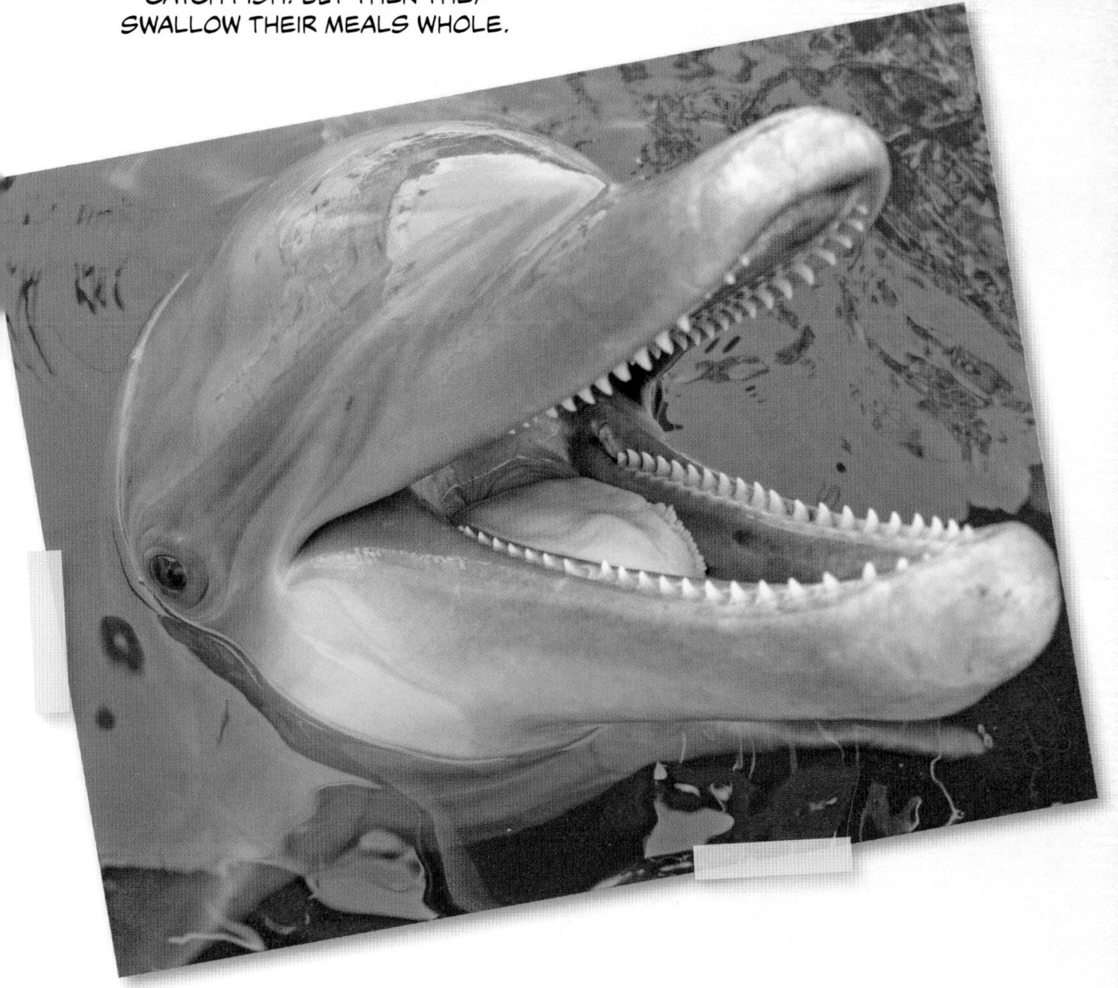

- Most adult dolphins grow to be 7 to 19 ft (2 to 3 m) long.
- Dolphins are usually black, white, or gray. They have two flippers on their sides and a triangular fin on their backs.
- Dolphins that live together talk to one another by using special sounds.
- Some dolphins can live for up to 30 years.

More Smart Dolphins

Researchers taught a dolphin named Kelly to search for litter in her **enclosure** and bring it to them. Each time she found a piece of litter, she got a fish to eat. Kelly soon figured out that the more litter she handed over, the more treats she got! So, she hid a piece of paper under a rock and tore off small pieces over and over again to take to her keepers!

Todd Endris, a Californian surfer, was on the water one day when a great white shark bit him. The surfer was in trouble. Just then, a pod of bottlenose dolphins appeared. They swam around Todd, forming a **barrier** between him and the shark. With the pod protection, the surfer was able to swim back to shore for help.

DOLPHINS ARE VERY INTELLIGENT ANIMALS THAT CAN BE TAUGHT A NUMBER OF SKILLS.

Glossary

agitated very stressed

barrier an obstacle between two areas or objects

currents water moving continuously in set directions

echolocation a method of finding objects by sending out sounds and listening for their echoes

enclosure an area set aside for an animal to live in

herd to round up or move a group of animals in a particular direction

mammals animals that give birth to babies and feed them with milk from their bodies

ordeal a stressful or upsetting event

pod a group of dolphins

predators animals that hunt and eat other animals

vital absolutely necessary

vulnerable at risk for experiencing harm

DOLPHINS LIVE IN PODS WITH UP TO 30 MEMBERS.

Index

Read More

Mattern, Joanne. *Dolphins (The World's Smartest Animals).* Minneapolis: Bellwether Media, 2021.

Murray, Julie. *Dolphins (Animal Kingdoms).* Minneapolis: Abdo Publishing, 2020.

Schuh, Mari. *Dolphins (The World of Ocean Animals).* Minneapolis: Jump!, Inc., 2022.

Learn More Online

1. Go to **www.factsurfer.com** or scan the QR code below.
2. Enter "**Pod Protection**" into the search box.
3. Click on the cover of this book to see a list of websites.